1

Blue Shades Publishing Inc.

380 Redwood Lane NW, Unit C

Concord, North Carolina 28027

www.blueshadespublishing.com

ISBN: 979-8-9887958-3-4

Book cover design by Abby Behrens

For the tenacious girls full of love...

In Her Early Twenties
By
Lindsey Bleu

Welcome to Your Twenties

The world seems to constantly
Shrink then expand
Inhaling as I discover who I am
Exhaling when I lose sight of her

It is the perfect blend of
Intimidation and wonder
That makes living so beautiful-
So worth it!

Knowing the world is breathing
Alongside of you
Gives this sense of camaraderie
In the changes all around us

Or within us...
For that is the change to focus on
Continued growth and newfound love
Budding relationships and building strengths

As we enter our twenties
Let's fill our days with
Endless discovery and
Have passion and sense mingle a bit

It's a wonderful world
When you notice
How wonderful the world is.
We are wonderful too.

Secret Petals

My heart has been captured
By a prince in these woods
I can't reach out to him
Don't know what I'd say if I could

My lips form the words
But to flowers they speak
Because to say these words to him
I am much to weak

The petals, they encourage
In their violets and yellows
But my stomach flutters
For what if it's not I who he chose

The leaves, they tell me
How it will all work out
"He's worthy of your love"
The stems seem to shout

With roses for eyes
The sun shines all day
Even when clouds appear
They never seem to stay

They only water the flowers
And help them grow strong
And with each storm that passes
We still get along

But I still come to the pasture
Where beautiful things grow
And let them remind me
Of what I already know

When I speak to my lovelies
And pour out my whispers of red
I imagine it's his ears
That have heard what I said

Oh, how I wish the flowers
That he confides in alone
Would pull him close and tell him
All that my flowers have known

But my confessions continue
And no secret is told
The petals of violets and yellows
Are the only hands I hold

Pacifist

I would like to be frozen in stone
Even if I had to watch
As the world moved around me

At least then I could be at peace
Knowing that I couldn't do anything
to stop it from all burning down

Home

I make his coffee
And he brings me my tea
That we drink in our sunroom
As the morning rays reveal the day

I give him a smile
And he shares his laugh
Then we both take one more sip
And lean back in our rocking chairs

I take his mug
And he waters my plants
Before we walk back into our kitchen
Where we dance with no music

I kiss his lips
And he hugs my waist
Until we breathe as one
Just as it's been since we found each other

For I am his
And he is mine
Though we roam untethered
Just two souls who share a home

And Then

And then one night
After the sun had already set
I poured out my day into my journal
But when I wrote his name
The pen curved in a new way,
The ink flowed heavier on the page
Than it had in the past

I'd written his name
probably 100 times in that book
And read it back twice more
This page, this line, *this* name
Was unrecognizable, yet
It was already attached to my heart
I knew it would be written a 1000 times more

Chokehold of Time

Hands gripped around my throat
Another second goes by
They twist

My heart pounds to the clicks
The little black ticks
Flood my vision

I cannot move without their grasp
We go together
Only one growing old

The less I say
The tighter the hands hold
The less I do

The more stuck I become
Slowly suffocating
From the hands of time

Quest for Love

When on the quest for love
One must first become a dreamer
Who traces hearts around names
Etched into a cedar table,
Finds joy in clouds against the blue sky,
Shares the dance of a rippling lake,
Sips warmth from a cup
Feeling the heat slide all the way down
Till it fills their stomach

One must love the feeling
Of a soft, warm towel
wrapped around their chest
Or the smell of laundry mixed with perfume
Buried inside the collar of their shirt
And seek the colors
Of this world that only exist in imagination,
Wander barefoot through the grass
While the sun draws freckles on their nose

One must bake fresh chocolate-chip cookies
To share with their neighbors
And offer a smile first
To the strangers on the street,
Leave doodles on the notes they write
Signing every entry with "love,"
In drunkenly, loopy handwriting

For the quest of love
Requires all the senses to come alive
Seeking out all lovable things
Within this world
So that one day, the one will find you
And you'll recognize their love in every form

But for right now
They are tracing hearts, looking at clouds,
And walking barefoot in the sun

Windy Day

He loves to play with my hair
Lifting it up high
Dropping it down onto my face

If he's feeling naughty
He'll put a hand under my skirt
As I blush and push it back down

In the summer, we fly kites
He blows gently on my neck
Bringing me scents of fresh cut grass

At night he taps on my window
Yelling for me to climb out
So he can sweep me off my feet again

In the fall, we go sailing
I let him do all the work and
He splashes me with the salty sea

At times he presses up against me
Weaving himself into my skin
Leaving my cheeks all rosy into the next day

He's always on the move
To places I can not go
It's hard to be in love with a windy day

Tethered

In love I am bound
But by love I am free

For countless loves
Have tied themselves to me

Still, I've remained untethered
With dispositions of glee

Now I use their thread
To tie myself to thee

Though you grasp at my line
You never pull me near

Now I am bound to you
But you're the one who steers

Dragging my head through clouds
Slipping poems into my ear

I could be pulled by you forever
Yet it is my greatest fear

Brown Eyes

He said he loved me.
I would have believed him, but
Then he told me my eyes are brown

When they are actually
The color of fallen pine needles
on a damp autumn day

He couldn't see how
They changed in the sun
Or the green that lives behind them

How their color holds power-
Flakes of gold drowned in honey,
Poured into a tree bark mug

So I didn't tell him that his eyes
Are the color of rich soil
That my eyes fall on

How they grow heavier, deeper
Brewing like coffee on a rainy day
Bringing comfort and a sense of forever

Instead, I let him believe
that both our eyes are
Brown.

Five of us in Total

There were five of us in total
Roaming the cobble streets
But when you tilted your head to talk
It was our eyes that would always meet

You knew you looked best in moonlight
So that's the time you chose
A flare for the grandeur of moments,
A mastermind of shows

The two of us walked together
Though five of us were there
I laughed at all your jokes
And ignored the other three's stare

When we made it to the fountain
And tossed a coin in
I wished to visit Rome once more
Just to see you again

Though I know it was not special
At least not in your eyes
But I will always remember those streets
With you and stars in the skies

And yes, I have been back since
With the romantic veil removed
Making me believe I must have dreamt it
The night five equaled two

Dawn

When you wake before the sun
Darkness invites you in
For a cup of tea-— two sugars please
His hands shake as he pours
And he talks deep and slow,
Pausing as he takes a sip

But his eyes are steady and bright
Like two stars in the dead of night
He fixes them on the window
That overlooks a garden on a hill
And watches as the light
Begins to lift her eyelids awake

"This is my favorite part"
Darkness says, low and drawn out,
"To see her rise, just for a moment.
To know she is still here"
But when I look back from the window
To see my new friend's face
He was already asleep, with his gaze on the horizon

Sublunary Love

If the moon beams
Were our two cans and a string
I would grab mine and
tell you "I adore you" every night
I'd use the stars up above
To paint my pictures of love
In images only you would know
Made of fiery light
Then I'd send a kiss
In the soft, night, wind
To land upon your cheek
the left, then the right
And when the sun will rise
She'll touch your eyes
To make all your days
Sunny and bright

For if I can not love you where you are
I'll recruit the world to do it for me

Mahogany and Wine

He smells like the kind of rich
Only a man could possess
But I felt safe wrapped up in it
like a comforter
Or a cloud

Or the warmth of red wine
As it rushes to your cheeks
And lands in the soft part of your belly
Makes your mind tingle
As your walls fall down

Mahogany and cigar ash
Mingle inside your nose
As your skin falls closer into his-
A whiff of his cologne does you in
And his legs replace the leather couch

It's a desire to experience him
But a chore to maintain
So as I sip from his glass
I contemplate his last name
And let my body rest in his riches

Daily

In the morning I want to hug my friends
I want to start the day by dancing
And I want to eat cereal on the balcony

In the afternoon I want to walk in the sun
I want to smile at strangers that pass
And I want to pick a flower from the grass

At night I want to laugh at dinner
I want to be wrapped in my fuzzy blanket
Mostly, I want to go to sleep madly in love

My Friend, Jesus

You are the mug that holds my tea
On a cold morning
Protecting me from the heat
Providing all the warmth I need

You make it easier to hold
All this world's troubles
Knowing that You will be between
All that could ever burn me

Verbal Warning

She speaks in bombs
And riddles

Her tongue could carry freight trains
Trained under the weight of the words
It flicked out to the world

Words that took years to create
Phrases that took generations

Her teeth were filed
As if to let each syllable slip unscathed
Through the perfect cracks

She dams up the words
She knows would damn people

Her mind collecting, like water for a rainy day
So when a flood is needed
She'd know just what to say

So she speaks in bombs
And in riddles

Her mouth turning at the corners
As she makes a turn of phrase
Undetected in her ways of destruction

Sending spies into the field
Stalking those, to hear

Her ears, her best accomplice
Compliant without fail
To concern themselves with the others' intel

She tries not to damage
Those who could not bear to know

Her smile hides her secrets
That aren't hers to be told
At least not yet...

Senseless

I sewed up my eyes
To escape your tender glances
And tightly shut my lips
So that they shall not reveal
My darkest secret, that everyone knows
Of the deepest, red, wine
Poured into two glasses, I hold
Waiting, desperate to be drunk
Waiting, patiently to be tasted

But the sewing can not prevent me
From remembering your eyes
And my lips are not needed to tell
All that I feel and desire to be felt
Not when, I stand beside the table
In the middle of a lonely room
With two glasses filled to the brim
And wait without senses
For you to take one from my hand

4 AM

Now it's four in the morning
I've awoken just to remember you

But you're sound asleep 200 miles away-
Dreams filled with all the clues

All the answers that I seek
In the shadows of my room

But it makes it harder to dream
Through the waking nightmares of me and you

Hesitations

I've been pausing
When I pour my tea
Letting the pitcher
Hang in my hand
Longer than it needs to

I get stuck
When I turn the page of a book
Feeling the pages
Rest against my skin
No word has been read

I stop in the middle
Of brushing my teeth
Just looking into the mirror
Trying to see
What other life I could be living

My days are full of hesitations
Hours growing with each task
That I parallel with
You being beside me
Just to compare

Just to dream
Just to dare
To imagine a place
Where you fill my silence
Waiting for you to return

We would just pick up
Where the scene ends
I fill your glass with tea
You read the paper next to me
We smile at each other through the mirror

I wait for you in the seconds
Of the day
To find your place in my life
Before I snap back to reality
My hesitations shortening each time

The Truth

Emotions reveal
Our thoughts' deepest lies
Unable to be controlled
Or rescripted

So while I think
"I'm still in love with him"
Closer inspection tells me
My heart has found its distance

Legality of Love

Love always feels illegal in the beginning
With suspicious looks from across the room
Subtle touches to not arouse suspicion
Hiding smiles behind hands

It feels forbidden to be in a world
Where only you two exist
Wondering if this intoxication is worthy of arrest
Knowing you'll eventually give in to the crime

Just Breathe

His breaths are loud and painfully slow
Sucking out my life as he pulls back
Then, proclaiming to be the hero
With every planted kiss
As if seeds of ecstasy were on his lips

My breaths are quiet in the dark room
Retreating with every movement
Of his hand on my body, his mouth towards mine
Letting my body take over
So my mind won't have to remember

His breaths become sharp- like daggers
The more of me he claims as his
Lingering there, marveling at the potential,
Awakening with every exhale

My breaths become loud in my ears
Though he didn't seem to hear through
the sound of my body crashing-
Into his, in and out of consciousness-

His breath touches my skin
Where clothes used to be
Marking his lips' next target

My breath begins to draw out
Like a bow without an arrow
Taking aim, nothing to release

His breath whispers fog into my ear
Of this satisfaction song

My breath comes back to me
I focus on his TV, still on, and

His breaths

My breaths

Please

I want to be able to close my eyes
Knowing that flashes of your hands
Won't form phantom touches on my skin
Or visions of your triumphant face won't appear

I want to smile and be kind
And it not entice you to think I'm okay
To think that you can be with me
As you were before, as you wish to again

I want to go about my day as normal
Without fear of running into you
Because you know my routine
And I won't respond to your messages

I want to dream at night
About the beauty of the world
Not those I am scared of
Or those I believe will protect me

I want to run away as far as I can
From your memory
Without leaving where I am now
So I can call it home again

I want you to take it as seriously as I am
To learn from it as I did
And to respect my decision
indefinitely, unquestionably, understandably

New Found Strength

I suffered in silence
Because I didn't know
What I thought
You deserved

Aware of the power
My words could have
On the trajectory
Of your life

Scared to admit
I was not as strong
As I needed to be,
As I thought I was

I suffered in silence
Because peace for you
Was still a question
But I was going to suffer anyway

It was the first time
I felt as though
My gentleness, my heart
Had betrayed me

But that was then
Now my story is told
And I've met a new form
Of strength

Our Father

The war that lived inside me
Was too big for me alone
So, when I collapsed on the battlefield

A voice told me to stay down
Obedient, desperate, I began to sleep
Until a truce was called within me

He scooped me up, that voice I heard
Nursed my heart,
Tended to my scratched up soul

Everyday He'd inch up the blinds
So that one morning my eyes awoken
To nothing but sunshine

Because that's the kind of
Father
Our God is

Moving on His own
While our body rests in His love, then
Blesses us with another day beyond our past

He gives us a chance to redefine
Our circumstance and sorrow
Gathering our pieces, to create new

Our Father,
A fierce protector of our hearts
A tender restorer of our peace

Never leaves us alone
Through any season of life
He stands all around us

When the weariness of war washes over you
Learn to rest in the battlefield
For your Father is there

Come with Me

I don't want to remember you the wrong way
The one that has holes
Where my memory slipped

I want to carry all of you with me
And it'd still be lighter than
Just carrying myself

White Paper

The white paper
Encroached by yellow of age
Dropped with coffee stains
Ink blots smeared by careless hands
Slurring the words across the page

Inch by inch losing its color
To the environment beyond itself
Never being able to erase the damage
Remembering how pristine it once was
Guarding what little white remains

Goodbye, I loved you

Four missed calls
Two missed texts
600 miles away

I can't help but wonder
What would've happened
If I'd had stayed

Though I can't change
Leaving, now
That I had left

But I know that
You are seeing all my
Calls and my texts

Each step I take
Towards you
I lose my direction

Lost and alone
Friendship of my own
Detriment of my action

So I'll stop reaching out now-
If I can force myself to do so-
So I can remember us politely

Single Oar

It is as though I woke up
To find myself in the middle of the sea
All alone, a single oar and me

And I asked questions of why and how,
Failing to make sense
Of my circumstance

Until I remembered climbing into the boat,
Untying the rope,
And pushing off the dock

I remember inching further from the shore,
Still keeping it in sight
Until one night, I rested in the waves

And awoke to nothing but blue sky,
murky water, and
The single oar next to me

How easy it was to be swallowed
By the seas persuasive tides, unaware
of the distance I've gained from home

How difficult it will be to row
Back to the lost shore with a single oar,
But oh, how I miss the land

Me

My lungs love the mountains
My skin desires the beach
My feet crave the Bluegrass
My heart sings for Italy
My spirit resides in Greece
My legs stretch for anywhere else
My mind dreams of the forest
My hands reach for dirt
My hair flows where it's breezy
My eyes indulge in the city
My fingers trace flower petals
My cheeks soak up the sun
My shoulders carry luggage
My ears delight in laughter
My lips praise the Lord
My stomach flutters for foreign
My body rests in home

Blackberry Bushes

Green to red to black
We waited patiently
For July
To bring blackberries back

Golden light
On climbing vines
That grow heavier
As berries begin to ripen

We pluck
Each one in its turn
Carefully dodging thorns
Letting juices stain our fingers

Fireflies steal
The sun's sweet glow
Playing hide-and-seek
Through the weeds

This is our cue
Night has come
To tend to her bushes
For tomorrow's harvest

Where our family
Wanders through fields
To see what the day
Has brought us

Never failing to provide
The tender fruit
Wrapped in armor
Ready to be reaped, again

That Feeling

Burrowed between my love
And biggest fear
A familiar face has appeared
I realized just how long it has been
Hiding from me, or I from it

Meeting once again,
Though it had grown mature in our time apart
I should've seen it sooner
So I could let it stay young
Instead, I put on a smile as it aged away

I wasn't ready to rekindle
My flame with loneliness
I was ashamed to meet it again
But here I am, sitting next to it
Telling both of us it will be okay

Secret Thorns

I write of flowers
A lot less than I used to
But one of my powers
Is still hopelessly searching for *you*

I'm not the same girl
Who started this quest
I've had a few bad twirls
And failed a few tests

But I promise to try
To find you before
I choose another wrong guy
Who leaves my heart feeling sore

If they didn't look so nice
And deceive me so well
I wouldn't look twice
And wouldn't have fell

Now my wall is up
So I can't trip again
But when the right one comes
I'll be sure to let him in

I have learned my lesson,
From which I have sworn
To double check all my flowers
For their secret thorns

New Tenant

You fill my mind with
White linens and natural light
Drawing curtains back
Replacing the flowers in my vases
Picking up fallen clothes
Leaving post-its on the mirror

You're making my mind
Lovely and clean
Restoring it back to its coziness
A place where laughter sings while
Candles dance in the corner
And the table is always full

You, with your ease and comfort,
Slowly patching up
The last tenant's damage
With every smile and question and memory
My mind begins to regrow
The garden that was just picked raw

Lost Words

Words in my head
Turn to words on a page
Yet sometimes I think
That they're not mine

Instead I stumbled
Upon them
As they escaped
Someone else's mind

So I scooped them up
To throw on a page
With other words that can be hard
For people to find

Hoping that their
Original creator would read
The words they had lost
And realize it will all be fine

Déjà Vu

A familiar gaze
Upon foreign eyes
Trick my brain
To thinking
It's you by my side

But it's not your soul
Just your spirit
That fills the air
This stranger and I
Now breathe together

He is not as daring
As you once were
But our silence
Builds bridges
All the same

Perhaps one day
He and I can
Meet in the middle
The way that we
Never could

River Red

I take all my paints
To the river by my house
Holding each in my hand
Before the cap is plucked
And color is dumped
Painting the river red
And blue and yellow and green
Purple, pink, brown, white, black

They collide together
Move together
Until they become one with each other
One with the current and the water
Blended individuals
Parted for so long
Finally making a mess of the art
They were supposed to live

Empty bottles littered around me
I sink to the grass
My hand rests on the red
It's too painful to hold
The blue, too slippery to grip
White, too muddy to recognize
Yellow, too heavy to pick up
I'll never be able to bottle them back up again

On My Shoulders

Lord up above
And down below
And right beside me

How Your hands are gentle
And warm upon my shoulders
Holding me up

My chin quivers as
Tears rush to my eyes-
I do not hold back

I do not say the words
Balanced on the tip
Of my tongue

Because You know, Lord
And You care
And You have more prepared

But You do not motivate
Me just yet,
You let me rest instead

In silence, we stand
Hands on my shoulders
You press me together again

Too Much to Ask For

There is the tragedy
That leads to art
It soon becomes
Romanticized, inconsequentially desired
Portrayed and distributed
Stretched to relatability
With this strange attachment
To holding onto the broken
Falling deeper into this perception
That we too are as tragic
As helpless, as tattered
As the art we consume

Then there is the art
In which we can never live in
Idealized, fantasized, envisioned-
But never obtainable
This art is not tragic
But lovely and whimsical
We oft give up a lot easier
On the art we want the most
And settle our minds
To the pitfalls of tragedy,
Accepting the ease of fall
Before daring to increase
Our distance from rock bottom

Indebted

Love is not cheap
It can be taxing on the heart
And some loves-
Perhaps the best loves-
Will have you in debt forever

Narrative Nuances

My story has been told
A thousand times through

The characters are known,
Plot begins to be predictable

Dialogue unchanged
Actions unwavering

Each time I hear
All that I have done

I nod my head
Like it's my first listen

I laugh on cue and
Cringe when necessary

It's never not compelling
This story of mine

But I am coming to realize
Just how unreliable the narrator is

Since Then

Since then
My tolerance for men
Has been shrinking

Then I began thinking
That tolerance shouldn't have to be
Measured every time I meet

Another guy
And they say "hi"
Then I have to check in

With myself, because I've been
In this position before
Where they make me think of more

Than just our conversations
Now I think of reservations
Doubts resurface at their mention

Wondering of their intentions
Until it's too late,
I'm not the girl they want to date

Because my walls are high
And they question the climb
While I question the fall

Could have been all
Avoided, we both could've had a win
But not a chance of that, since then

Stained Glass

Sometimes you can be clear as glass
And people will still look at you
Like you're a stained window

Choosing their own patterns-
Calling themselves mesmerized
While playing master of the colors

they use to distort your reality.
With rose colored glasses
Or envious green shades

Ruining the attempt of an authentic self
Giving each stranger, friend, and lover
The title of artist over your life

Blunt, honest, sweet, and resolved
There's no dissuading them of their vision...
They've already put it in their church

So Much Potential

I've slaughtered identities
Thinking inner-me's were enemies
Leaving villages of dreamers
Left to hide

Society talks about potential
And how I'm not using it
So another part of me dies-
I push it to the side

My dreams have cowered
As I reaped them one by one
Stacking them up
Thinking they have died

But a heart still beats
Deep within each of my dreams
A rhythm that knocks
A soul to bide

Potential doesn't leave
When you turn your back on a dream
It waits for you where you left it
Withstanding every tide

Who Am I

Who am I,
But a girl
Trying to validate
Her own opinions

Not as fact,
But as true
Not to anyone
But herself

Who am I,
But a human
Trying to understand
The world

Not through lessons
But through senses
Not through pain
But through love

Who am I,
But a part of nature
Trying to coexist
With all I am not

Not with force
But with emotion
Not with selfishness
But with compassion

Who am I,
But God's child
Trying to live
As He wishes me to

Not as flesh,
But as daughter
Not as sinner,
But as saved

Who am I,
But a girl,
A human, a part of nature and
Daughter of the King

This Year

This year was written
In bold, capital letters
Each word holding depth
Drowning the pages
Until I thought I couldn't
Hold my breath,
Any longer

This year was a demolition
Of the house
I worked so hard to build,
Stripped down to only the bones
Exposed to every element
It would've crumbled
If not for the *firm* foundation

This year was a harvest
Where my hands
Were always caked in soil
As I dug up the crops
I would use to
Get me through the
Desolate winter

This year was a forest fire
Sweeping through foliage
Consuming all in its path
The trees screaming
In sizzling silence
Awaiting the day their seeds
Will replenish what was lost

This year was a choreographed dance
Of every emotion I could feel,
Each in a leotard of their own color
Weaving around on the stage
I, their lone observer,
Watching the chaos ensue,
Trying to call it all art

The Pea

My body is a year removed,
My mind survived decades
Of emotions since.
I've stacked memories
On top of each other,
And climbed to the top,
But even with layers of comfort
Sometimes rest still doesn't come easily.

My body is a year removed
And it's stood in front of
Hundreds of mirrors,
Yet each might as well
Have been shattered
As my soul failed to recognize
The woman that stood before it.
But, over time I became reacquainted
Fragment by fragment.

My body is a year removed
From the moment that now only exists
In seconds my mind allows it to.
Though the time passes faster
Than they did six months ago
And faster still than nine.
Maybe after today, day 365,
I won't need to count them anymore.

Softer

There's a softer
version of me
just below the surface

She's what I'd imagine
A cloud to feel like
(But) wrapped in armor

Designed by myself
So she doesn't
Float away

For who would
Hold my heart, if not
Her billowing hands?

I almost lost her once.
As she sought
For her own protector

Guided by light
But she caught the attention
Of pure fire instead

He absorbed a piece of her
And a hole still remains
But she is safe again, with me

This softer version of me
Ensures that my heart
Knows why it still beats

A role too important
To just let her float away
So I keep her tucked inside

Until the right person,
Whose softer version is in control,
Picks up the shield with honor

Love Without Meaning

I am sorry
I could not recognize
The depths of your love for me.
I easily felt gratitude for it,
And could recite the actions
Behind your emotion
But it was impossible
For me to internalize.

Perhaps I feared losing
What I think I did not deserve
So I thanked you profusely
Without ever letting myself
Acknowledge its meaning.
So that when the inevitable
Happened I could bear it more easily

Why I Write

Maybe I write because
I fear being forgotten
Recognizing moments
Don't always turn into memories
When I am in them, for people

Not because I was not loved,
Maybe not for any reason at all
Other than it is human nature
To forget those who leave
Over time, losing their presence

Maybe that's why I run
Once the poem is written,
Forever immortalizing their love
Before erasing myself from their mind
Never to meet again

Not because I wanted to leave
Maybe because I feared they would first
Then suddenly syllables of flowers would
Become stanzas of despair
But I have the choice to not let it get there

Maybe that's why I call
The people I love so much
Losing myself in the past
Pulling them there with me
Even just for a 15 minute chat

Not out of pure love-
Although that is part of the reason-
But because I want them to love me
Like they once did,
When we weren't so far apart

Maybe that's why...
Battling the question, resting on a pendulum.
What is easier to bear?
Being forgotten,
Or sticking around to see if I would be?

Of Tongue and Page

I often think about your words
How an entire world
Balances on the edge of your tongue
You swallow it back
When it's your turn to listen
Collecting the syllables
Of another, especially you admire,
Adding them to your universe

I think our words differ
From each other
Because I write as if to speak
But you speak as if to write
What a beautiful reversal
We have choreographed
I often think about your words and
Imagine the ink trail- cranberry colored usually-
They leave as they bleed into the air

As plants and humans breathe
Our words trace over each other
Briefly, before being collected back
To tongue and page
Making conversation contain
Multiverses of the lives we speak and write
Then pause, until the next world is revealed

Love, the Novel

You spoke "love" as a word
But I read it like a novel

Day and Night

Like the sun and moon above
I'll sedate my love until I find you

Who is to say
That day and night are not in love?

For how can you explain the passion
As they become a single embrace

A collision of art, whispers of pink
With tangerine strokes

Spending their whole lives
Chasing after the other

Only to slip away out of their arms once more
Moon or morning rise

Day's crown of sun rays
Night's armor of stars

Taking turns to search the world
Only to catch a glimpse of each other

Their emotions stored up
Then released along the sky

Sedated love, alive at last
Merely by the vision of one another

How could that not be
Considered the greatest love of all?

Baby Blue Nail Polish

In the summer
I paint my toes baby blue
Because I like the way it looks
Against the green grass,
Or up against the sand,
Or underneath the water

I like how the color
Captures a piece of the bright sky
And seems to glow more
As my skin darkens over the days
Or when I wear white sandals
With the straps that wrap around my ankles

I feel so human
When a piece chips off
And I sit on my bathroom counter
Or the edge of my bed
And I gently fill it in again
Covered in a clear coat

I won't allow myself
To paint my toes blue
Any other time of year,
Afraid it will rob me of the joy from
that first warm day as the season changes

And I get to paint my toes baby blue, again

S'mores and the Lord

Lord, it smells like s'mores outside right now
All sweet and charred
And I don't see the fire that
I know loved ones are gathered around
But I want to thank you anyway,
For the sunshine
That created this warm weather
And the jobs
That funded the cheap bag of marshmallows
And the people gathered around the fire
That are probably laughing and talking
And telling the others
That they have the best roasting methods

Lord, I thank you for the smell of s'mores
Because you've given me the experience
Of making them myself
Because I know that soon
I too
Will be gathered around an open flame
Struggling to open a chocolate wrapper
With sticky fingers
As my friend waits (im)patiently for my stick
And the heat presses against
My sun-kissed cheeks
Oh lord, how I love you
For the smell of s'mores

Drinking for Two

You sit there
Pouring water into a net
I used to put my hand out
Just to be nourished by it

I'd wait for each drop
While streaming my water into you
As you screamed of your thirst
I'd take yours from me and give it to you too

I can never speak of my waters
Because it turned your heart blue
Maybe it was from how full
You were from drinking for two

Riddler's War

I guess I'm just confused
Because you asked a question
Then I gave an answer
Then you smiled
Before you disappeared

Was it not rhetoric?
When you asked me
What you did.
Was it not what you wanted?
When I answered what I said.

If I could go back
I'd sit silent by your side
Letting question marks float by
Knowing what would happen
If I were to speak

Giving a mischievous smile
But letting you know no more
So your questions would keep coming
I'd play the riddler's war
Just to go back to when I thought you were mine

Show Canceled

Oh, here we go again
Pricked by thorns to put me in a trance
Trying to be crazy in love
Only to wind up delusional in romance

Slipping syllables
Into his mouth then
Applauding his improvisation
Before stamping my own script
On a duetted conversation
Calling it art,
Living for the dramatics
While convincing my heart
Of its reality
Never to see the curtains open
Posters faded and worn thin
Yet the press always seems to get word
Writing their anticipatory reviews
Mostly calling it absurd

"Another love story
Untold by yours truly"
Headlines love to remind me
Of all the lines I wrote
Then had to erase
The empty seats
empty sets
empty scenes without a place
"Delusionally a masterpiece,
Expectedly a disaster piece"
They wait for the failure I'm sure to endure
The biggest pain
Being how correct my critics are
Or maybe it's still
That my true love is so far-
Away from reach

Rose petals on the floor
From flowers never thrown
I sit center stage
And direct the plays never shown

Nevermind

My mind was made up

But that didn't matter

Once our eyes met

Summer Storm

The storm rolled in suddenly
Veiling a perfect, blue sky
I was sitting on my porch and watched
The moment the sky began to cry

Slow at first, like it questioned its grief
Then the anger set in
And a tantrum spread
Quickly through the land

Lightning struck
Through her tears into the earth
Thunder haunted the air
With its low, sorrowful, song

I wondered what rage could the sky have?
If I could calm her soul with a simple word-
CRACK! My thoughts were interrupted
As I watched a tree rip in half

Branches that could swallow me whole
Lay scattered across the ground
The trunk mourned softly above its loss
And the sky cried harder at its destruction

It felt silent, though I heard the whole thing
From the crying and cracking and crashing
My porch became solemn as I learned
The sky gets sad and trees die too

12:01 AM

I talked to you
Until tomorrow
So much
I lost track of
What today is
Just as yesterday
And next week...
Possibly forever

Just a Dream

I took a nap today
It was all I could do
To keep from telling you
I love you

But there you were
In a dream I made
Where I confessed my feelings
Then woke up the same

Are you sure
You didn't hear me?
When I told you
While I slept.

I am sure
That I meant it.
So, if you could
Please just say it back

In a dream
Or wide awake
Though the latter
Would be preferred

Not that it really matters
What you have or haven't heard
When it was all
Just a lovely dream

Ghost Love Story

To watch red cheeks
Slowly regain color

Or wide, beautiful eyes
Shrink once more

Eyes that used to seek each other
Finding another or the floor

To stand a little further
When we're talking

Noticing how full the room is
When its occupants used to be just two

To lose butterflies
Born of a smile

Or the mention of a name
(How addicting a name can be)

I don't want to watch you
Fall out of love with me

Before we even get the chance
To see what love for us could be

I don't want to absorb
So much of you

Just to watch you fade away
Without ever actually leaving the room

The room will never be the same
It'd see too much to restore

I don't want-
I can't have-

I really wish to not watch
As I fall victim to another ghost love story

Shrinking the World

I told you a story about my sister
Then you called her by name

It was like the first time I ever heard it
Each syllable swelled in my ears

Before I knew it I was smiling
When did you start collecting such knowledge?

What a weapon of intimacy that was!
How armed are you?

My mind was racing with all I knew about you
And everything I wanted to find out

It's one of my favorite feelings, you know
When you feel the world shrink just a little

August Began

August began with a Tuesday
How perfectly balanced
A Tuesday can be
In a week of chaotic days

I swam through the air
Welcoming it into my lungs
Knowing by Thursday it will be,
Ever so slightly, crisper

August's first day saw the sun
Fall a little faster than July
A little slower than September will
But what a show each month presents

August began with a Tuesday
And peanut butter toast for breakfast
And a new route to work
From a new apartment

I think I really like August
Feelings growing
Just in time for harvest
Where I will store them until next month's desires

Warm

You're warm like
A fire in the distance
Withholding the part of you
That would burn me
Staying close enough
For me to slowly melt
Making me forget my scars
From fires
That weren't as considerate
As you

On my way to work

He was wearing a sweater
In the heat of a Carolina June
Chocolate colored
Which told me he was sweet
With a white button down underneath
Which told me he was sophisticated
Dark curly hair and darker rimmed glasses
Framed his face perfectly
He was walking to work
But belonged in a library
Or one of those coffee shops
That served lattes in a real glass
Or even Italy
With a cigarette loose in his hand

A Poet

For others I have found
Beautiful words to craft into stanzas

I've twisted language to convey
Who they are to me

But not for him
No, he was full of poetry
Long before we met

In the way he turns a door knob
The shape his lips take
When he's speaking on his passions
The sound his steps make, growing nearer

Its stitched into the clothes he wears
Once they touch his skin
Or the curls of his hair against the wind

It pours out of him
Yet, he never runs dry

He is made of poetry
So for him, I don't have to try

But Gravity

An ode to the moon-
Conductor of the tides
Vault of the world's secrets
Watchful eye of her children

Always steady
Through every cycle
She ascends on schedule
Every time

Weepers of the night
Comforted by her presence
Heard through her beams
Rest peaceful below her

Yet few speak of Gravity
That ties them to her
Makes her so alluring
Giving her power to fulfill her destined role

Without gravity
The tides would have no pull
Nor the world be so sustained
Our precious moon would float

Helplessly through space
Hopelessly through time
Awaiting the day she'd be pulled close
To her destiny once more

Green

I fell in love with green
About two years back
It was just after spring
The world flooded in its hues

I would take naps in the grass
No blanket laid down
Beneath the dogwood
In my yard

Though the leaves pressed against
A bright blue sky
It was green
That wrapped me up, tight

I let my hands pick up blades
Then sprinkle them back
Down to the ground
Like confetti

An offering of my new favorite color
An expression of desire
For it to never fade
But eventually the world dulled into browns

I have not felt
That love for green
Since that year...
Until now...

Beach Required

I love coming to the beach
Where the salt wind
Plays with my hair
And sun rays
Paint roses on my skin
And the waves
Let me rise and fall with them

Kingdoms of sand castles
Built and destroyed in a day's time
While birds watch above us
Looking for their next meal
And all I'm required to do
Is lay in between it all and
Let myself be consumed by nature

I never leave the beach the same
I've been smoothed out
Covered with God's beautiful creation
Filled with a restful disposition
I let my eyes close to breathe in
Ocean's breath one last time
Sending a kiss back through my exhale

Suddenly

Suddenly, it happened
I began to experience
All the beautiful
Thoughtful things
I saw in him

Unedited

He is perhaps the first guy
To not make me feel rewritten

That's how I know he'll be the first man
I will allow myself to truly love

Lord, let them

Let them chase
After You
More than they chase
After the flesh of the other

Let them grow together
As they learn more
About each other, the world
And Your creations

Let them be filled
By You daily
Then pour into
One another

Let them find rest
In Your hands
And strength in the
Assurance of the other

Let them be joyful
In the love
You led them to
In Your perfect time

Let them love
As You have loved
With sacrifice and forgiveness
Given freely to each other

Let their minds stimulate
Bodies satisfy
And souls merge
In the purest love

The Head, The Heart, and the Healer

He is composed
Of all the good
From my poems past

Playing the antithesis
Of men who left,
What I thought would be, scars, forever

Yet I've been given new skin
From his loving hands
And his gentle heart

With qualities worth the wait
I know God has heard
All my prayers

Sending me the man
I would fall for, repeatedly
Never receiving a scratch

My heart has failed me
In times such as these
When intoxicated incorrectly

But now he guards it
In the softness of his soul
So my head may heal the rest of me properly

The head, the heart, and the healer
Each of them myself
Each of them my Love

Ugh, Poetry

I fear to write about you

You already have too much power
Without me immortalizing you (again)
But I also can't say it to you
So my options are thin
On where to put all of these emotions-
To shout my truth
Or whisper my desires
(Though sometimes those two should be flipped)

I don't know whether to tell you
That I love you (or I hope I get the chance to try)

How else can I show you
The colors you make me see

You wouldn't understand the way I'd
Wait for you, pray for you and stay for you
(perhaps unconditionally)

I can not tell you this (some is likely known)
So one day the world will burden my reality
Some will surely pity
A girl so in love
Most will understand
The heartache of an unheld hand
But I will curse myself
That they may know you at all

Not when, I'm sure, I'll still wish to call you mine

Bibles Belong

Bibles belong on the floor
When your knees meet it there
Or you're lying on your belly
With your feet up in the air

Bibles belong on stained coffee tables
Where life gets messy sometimes
Or cluttered bedside tables
For when sleep is hard to find

Bibles belong in nervous, sweaty hands
When words are too blurry to read
Bibles belong in confident, steady hands
When you use The Word to lead

Bibles belong anywhere
That we choose to go
The most high renowned places
Or the lowest of low

Bibles belong with us
A gift from our giving God
So bring your Bible with you
Even if it feels odd

(My) Terrible Timing

Terrible timing
In which we have met
Have led to confessions
I'd rather forget than regret

Your garden had roots
That I failed to see
Even when you spoke of them
It was hard to believe

So I pushed my own timeline
And tried to draw you near
Telling you I adore you
To make losing me your biggest fear

Because you have no thorns
I wanted you all to my own
Then a voice began to tell me
To leave you alone

For a garden can not be
Reaped before it is sown
So I'm sorry for trying to harvest
Before fully grown

If I truly love you-
As I believe that I do-
I must let my terrible timing subside
And simply be there for you

I'll let you tend to your weeds
(While I tend to my own)
Putting my full trust back
Into God's timing alone

And if it's not you
That He has planned for me
I just want to thank you
For showing me your garden's beauty

You'll always have an admirer
Until your flowers' end
A supporter, a believer
And above all, a friend

Goodbye, Sunshine

Though the sun was setting
I sat in it drinking every last drop
As it told me stories of the day
I let it hold me
Even when I knew it was saying goodbye
Hoping the warmth collected
In the time of the light
Would last me well into
The dark and cold of night
And when my skin began to burn
I smiled knowing
I'll have more than just memories
To keep it with me
I had absorbed a piece of the sweet sun
Then let it rest
As the next phase of life begun
Anticipating to see the daylight once more-
The moon a constant reminder
Of its rays of warmth
The stars a glimpse of hope
For what the night will be worth
I promise to keep the sunshine with me
After it fades away
I promise to embrace the night
Until the next light of day
I pray that when it comes

It will choose to stay
Bending the laws of nature
Just to be with me in any way
So as I sat in the fading sun
Watching the world transform
I smiled for knowing it
And let the next phase be born
Goodbye, my gentle sunshine
Hello, the starlight of unknown
Let us embrace for a little bit
And be thankful for true colors shown

Your Early Twenties

Your early twenties
Are for knitting a sweater
Occasionally you'll unravel
Trying to start again
You might break a needle
Or damage the spool
Change your mind on colors
Or patterns, fabric or stitch
You'll get excited and try it on
Before it's fully done
Maybe seeing the potential
Or focusing on the incompleteness-
Then live in those emotions for a bit

One day you'll finish it
Expecting it to last well
Into your thirties
Then you'll realize
You can make a better one
So you start from scratch,
But you don't start with nothing
You'll use all the lessons
From the sweater before
Sitting cross-legged on the floor
In the fabric of
Your early twenties

About Author

I am a simple farm girl from central Kentucky, who was in fact "raised in a barn." Then, somewhere between the first and last poem of this book, I moved to North Carolina. I have always been blessed with wit, had an adoration of language and a habit of wearing my heart on my sleeve, making it only a matter of time before my first poem was written. I began writing in high school- though I didn't tell anyone (except my dear friend Claire) until much later. Instead, I am more known for hosting dinner parties, taking photos, traveling often, laughing loudly, and loving deeply. It wasn't until I started sharing more of my work that I realized that my gift can bring a relatable comfort to those unable to find words for themselves. Finding it nearly impossible to fit all my thoughts on a page alone, I figured a book would suffice. So, we've landed here, with all my vulnerabilities exposed, I am now officially an open book.

Acknowledgement

This book would not be possible without the blessings of so many friends and family. I would like to thank my Mom and Dad, Julia and Bleu Rice, for being my biggest cheerleaders through life. They have given me full trust as I stretch my wings and full comfort to fly home when needed. A special thank you to Claire Elise Schilder, who envisioned this book long before I did. Without her listening ear and consistent encouragement, this book would probably continue to be in the Notes app on my phone. Sarah Eifert for her belief in my talents and ability to understand me so completely. Abby Behrens for bringing visual beauty through the cover art and her support through the years. Above all, my full gratitude goes to my Lord and Savior Jesus Christ for His unfailing friendship, guidance and forgiveness. He was there for the entire story and the sole reason I made it through it all.

: @bylindseybleu

: @inherearlytwenties@gmail.com